Two Homes, One Heart

Bedtime Healing Meditation for Children

Little Blue Zen

Two Homes, One Heart

Copyright@ 2024 Jo Galloway

The right of the author has been asserted to her following the copyright writing, designs and patent act of Australia.

All rights reserved. No part of this book may be reproduced, stored or transmitted by any means whether auditory, graphic, mechanical, or electronic without the written permission of the author. Unauthorised reproduction of any part of this work is illegal and is punishable by law.

Unless otherwise noted, the author and the publisher make no explicit guarantees as the accuracy of the information contained in this book may differ based on individual experiences and context

ISBN: 978-1-7635801-9-0

Published by Little Blue Zen
Birdwood NSW
Printed in Australia
Cover Design: Gagan Karunachandra
Editing: Kristine Gibson
jo@littlebluezen.com
http://www.littlebluezen.com

Two Homes, One Heart

Bedtime Healing Meditation for Children

Jo Galloway

Your child may like other books in this series

- Bully Proof. Keeping out the bullies.

- I am Different, I am Me.

- The Magical Treasure Hunt. Building Confidence.

- The Magical Worry Balloon.

- Angelic Dreams. Meet your Guardian Angel.

- Scared of the Dark.

- I Love School.

- A Coat of Flying Colours

- Bedwetting, Dry Nights

INTRODUCTION

Why Healing Meditations.

As children we make sense of our experiences based on our limited understanding and perception. We may misinterpret events or draw conclusions that form the basis of limiting beliefs that influence our entire life. These beliefs become ingrained over time, shaping our thoughts, feelings and behaviours well into adulthood unless consciously challenged.

In my work as a practising Hypnotherapist, I've found that all my clients' concerns, whether rooted in fears, feelings of inadequacy, addictive behaviours, or other challenges, trace back to their early childhood experiences, interactions, and upbringing. It's important to note that these issues don't exclusively stem from abusive or dysfunctional environments; limiting beliefs can arise from various circumstances.

Parents or caregivers wield substantial influence in shaping our perceptions of ourselves and the world around us. Remarks, criticisms, or comparisons made by family members can foster beliefs about our capabilities, worthiness, or potential.

Furthermore, interactions with peers, teachers, and authority figures also contribute to the formation of these beliefs. Repeated experiences of rejection or failure can solidify beliefs such as "I'm not good enough" or "I'm unworthy of love."

This realisation ignited my passion for intervening at the source: working with children to prevent these beliefs from taking root and manifesting into significant challenges in adulthood. By addressing issues early on, we can guide children to develop into the best versions of themselves, free from the burden of limiting beliefs that could otherwise dominate their lives.

How Healing Meditation will help your child.

Teaching children meditation offers a multitude of benefits that can positively influence their daily lives and overall development. A regular mindfulness meditation practice provides valuable tools for managing stress, navigating emotions, and promoting overall well-being. Healing meditations, in particular, bolster your child's self-belief, helping to remove any resistance they may face in adulthood. This leads to a happier, more successful and fulfilling life.

Unlike traditional meditation, which often centres on relaxation, healing meditations go a step further by focusing on recovery, balance, and reprogramming a child's self-belief. These meditations use techniques such as breathing exercises, visualization, and guided imagery to not only foster deep relaxation but also reshape their mindset.

This targeted approach helps build a stronger sense of self-confidence and resilience. By integrating positive affirmations and emotional healing, healing meditations offer a distinct advantage over traditional methods, laying a powerful foundation for a child's future success and well-being.

Meditation can also be an effective part of your child's bedtime routine, helping to calm the mind and prepare the body for restful sleep. Techniques like guided imagery and deep breathing, as outlined in this book, can signal to the brain that it's time to wind down.

Sharing these calming moments at bedtime not only strengthens the bond between parent and child, but also creates a supportive and nurturing environment. It also sets a positive example, emphasizing the importance of self-care and mindfulness.

With patience and consistency, you can help your child develop a lifelong practice that supports their mental, emotional, and physical health. Give your child the gift of relaxation and imagination with this easy-to-read story designed to inspire and uplift.

Two Homes, One Heart

In this comforting and supporting tale, your child will meet Teddy, a gentle bear who offers comfort and understanding during times of family change. As Teddy holds your little one's hand and shares his soothing tale, he introduces two old trees, Oak and Willow, who learn that sometimes growing apart is necessary for happiness.

With warmth and kindness, Teddy reassures children that while changes at home can be unsettling, they also open the door to new adventures. He gently explains that even if parents live in different homes, their love for their child remains constant and unbreakable.

Through his heartfelt words, Teddy encourages children to embrace their feelings, helping them understand that it's perfectly normal to feel a mix of emotions during transitions.

This enchanting story provides a safe space for your child to explore their feelings about separation or divorce.

Teddy emphasises that their parents' love is forever and that, no matter how family dynamics shift, they are cherished and supported.

Perfect for bedtime, "Two Homes, One Heart," not only helps ease anxieties but also fosters open conversations about family changes. As your child drifts off to sleep with Teddy by their side, they'll find comfort knowing that love is the greatest treasure of all.

Best read slowly in a calm, steady voice. The more often your child listens, the more magical the results will be,

Little Blue Zen

Two Homes, One Heart

Hello, my precious Little Starlight.

It's time to leave the day behind and float into a peaceful magical world, where Teddy is waiting with a special story just for you.

But before we begin, Teddy wants to be sure you're feeling extra comfy tonight.

So, go ahead, have a little wriggle, and find the perfect spot.

When you're ready, let's take a nice big stretch.

Reach out your arms, your legs, your fingers and your toes.

Take a big deep breath in through your nose, then breath out through your mouth, as if you're blowing out all your birthday candles.

Perfect! Let's try that again, shall we?

Slowly take a deep breath in, hold, then breathe out.

"One more time," says Teddy.

Breathe in, hold, breathe out.

Now lying very, very still, softly close your eyes.

Did you know you can see perfectly well with your eyes closed, because all boys and girls have the most amazing ability to imagine things way better than grown-ups?

So, using your brilliant imagination, I want you to picture a ladder in front of you.

A shimmering golden ladder, with each step painted in the vibrant colours of a rainbow.

Each step sparkles as it catches the starlight from above.

The ladder reaches high into the sky.

"Let's climb up," says Teddy.

Taking a deep breath, you step onto the first step.

The colour is a rich ruby red, glowing warmly beneath your feet.

Then, you glide to the next step, a vibrant, juicy orange that feels like sunshine on your skin.

Each step is warm and inviting, lifting you higher into the sky.

Up you go, feeling more relaxed and sleeper with every step you take.

Next, you step onto a bright, dazzling yellow step, and suddenly your arms and legs feel all loose and floppy, like a rag doll.

With a deep breath and easy stretch, you effortlessly rise onto the lush green step.

Gentle sounds around you bring a sense of peace and calm.

You're feeling sleepier and sleepier with every step you take.

As you rise higher, you feel lighter,

as though you're drifting peacefully along on a soft, gentle breeze.

You gracefully step up onto the deep blue step, as a wave of excitement washing over you.

You're almost at the top, and Teddy is right behind you, his presence comforting and warm.

You reach the violet step, and with one last leap, you land softly on a fluffy white cloud.

Feeling very sleepy, you sit down, and Teddy snuggles up beside you.

Teddy squeezes your hand gently, his eyes twinkling with kindness.

"Are you ready to hear my special story?" he asks, his voice as soothing as a soft lullaby.

You nod, feeling safe and snug.

"This is a little story about two old trees that lived in the magical forest," he began.

"Their names were Oak and Willow."

"For years, they grew side by side."

"They loved sharing sunshine and shade, but as they grew, they realised they needed different things to thrive."

"Oak needed more sunlight, while Willow preferred the cool shade of other trees."

"One day, they talked about it and decided it was best for them to grow in different parts of the forest."

"They needed different things to continue to grow and be happy," explains Teddy.

"That is what's happening with your Mummy and Daddy," he whispers softly.

"Just like Oak and Willow, your Mummy and Daddy are finding what they need to be their best selves," Teddy says gently, his voice warm and reassuring.

"I know things at home are changing," he says, and sometimes, change can feel a little scary, especially when we don't know what's happening."

He paused, taking a deep breath.

"But remember, life is a big adventure!"

"There are twists and turns, and while some parts might seem a little frightening, there are also so many exciting new things to discover!"

"Your Mummy and Daddy have been going through a tough time, and they haven't been as happy as they usually are."

"So, they have decided that it's best for them to live in two different homes for a while, just like Oak and Willow."

"But here's the important part: this isn't a bad thing."

"Change can open the door to new adventures!"

"Even though you may have two homes now, I'll be with you no matter where you go."

"We will have two cozy beds, one at Mummy's house and one at Daddy's house and I'll snuggle with you at both places," smiles Teddy.

"We'll have the chance to make special memories in both homes."

"And guess what?"

"Now you get to have two birthday parties and two Christmas celebrations."

"One at Mummy's house and one at Daddy's house, double the fun!"

"Won't that be cool?" laughs Teddy.

"You'll get some extra special time with just Mummy or just Daddy, and you'll still have all your favourite toys with you!"

"Both homes will feel like home in no time!"

"Your Mummy will always be your Mummy, and your Daddy will always be your Daddy till the end of time."

"Nothing will ever change that, no matter where they live," Teddy explains.

"Sometimes, adults just need a little time to figure things out on their own."

"Remember," says Teddy, "they care about you deeply, but they're working through some big emotions right now."

"Your Mummy and Daddy might not always agree, but their love for you will always remain strong."

"You are their greatest treasure," says Teddy.

"You are very important to them and your happiness matters."

Teddy leans in closer, his voice barely above a whisper.

"Just because your Mummy and Daddy are having a hard time at the moment doesn't mean they're falling out of love with you."

"Your Mummy and Daddy's love for you is forever."

"Sometimes, grown-ups have to make hard choices that can be difficult to understand."

"They might have problems they can no longer fix together, no matter how many times they try," explains Teddy.

"Sometimes, the choices that grown-ups make can help them feel happier and be better parents."

"Remember, this is something between your Mummy and Daddy."

"They are separating not because of anything you did, but because they need to find their own way to be happy,"

"Please believe me Little Starlight."

"Even if your Mummy and Daddy are no longer together, they will always be your family."

"The chains of love that hold you together can never, ever be broken."

"Their love for you is bigger than the highest mountain."

"No matter what is happening at home, your Mummy and Daddy's love for you will always be there." assures Teddy.

"Because the love between a parent and a child is a different kind of love, a very special love that stands the test of time."

Teddy snuggles closer.

"I know you wish you could fix things between your Mummy and Daddy, but sometimes grown-up situations can be tricky, and there's nothing you could have done to change it," he says softly.

"It's okay to feel a mix of emotions, and remember, this is not your fault."

"Your Mummy and Daddy still love you very much, no matter what is happening between them."

Teddy looks at you with kind eyes.

"You are special, their greatest creation," he says warmly.

"There's no need to worry."

"What's important to remember is that you don't have to choose sides."

"Your Mummy and Daddy know you love them both very much."

"Right now, your Mummy and Daddy might seem a little distant or sad," he whispers.

"Occasionally, when people are upset, they say things they don't really mean, just like when you're feeling frustrated, you might say something that you really didn't mean to say."

"But that's okay!" assures Teddy.

"It's just part of what they're going through and how they're feeling."

Teddy smiles softly.

"Remember, time has a way of healing many things, and in the end, everything will be alright, you'll see."

"It's perfectly normal to feel a bit confused, and it's okay to feel sad or angry too," he adds.

"I'm here to listen whenever you need to talk, even if it's just in whispers," says Teddy.

"You can share your thoughts and feelings with me anytime."

"You're never alone, my little friend."

Teddy gently squeezes your hand.

"I will always be here to support you!"

"You'll still be able to do all the special things you love," Teddy says with a smile.

"Your Mummy and Daddy will always be there to support you and cheer you on!"

"No matter where you call home, whether it's one place or two, your family shares one heart, now and forever."

Teddy reaches out and gives you a soft, comforting hug.

"Your family might look a little different now, but you're still a family.

"Your Mummy and Daddy will always be there to support you, no matter what," Teddy says, giving you another warm, reassuring snuggle.

"Whenever you feel scared or unsure, just remember that I am here for you, ready to cuddle and listen," whispers Teddy.

You take a big sigh, letting Teddy's words wash over you like a gentle wave.

Each word surrounds you with warmth, reminding you that love is always present, no matter what happens or where you are.

As the clouds wrap you in their loving arms, a wave of sleepiness washes over you.

With Teddy by your side and all the love surrounding you, you can now gently, calmly, easily drift off to sleep.

When you wake up, you'll feel happy, safe, and full of love.

"Together, we can face any changes and find joy in all the new adventures ahead," says Teddy with a smile.

"And remember, your Mummy and Daddy will always love you."

"Some things might change," say's Teddy, "but love, love stays the same."

Sleep tight tonight, my wonderful little Starlight.

Sweet dreams.

Also by Jo Galloway

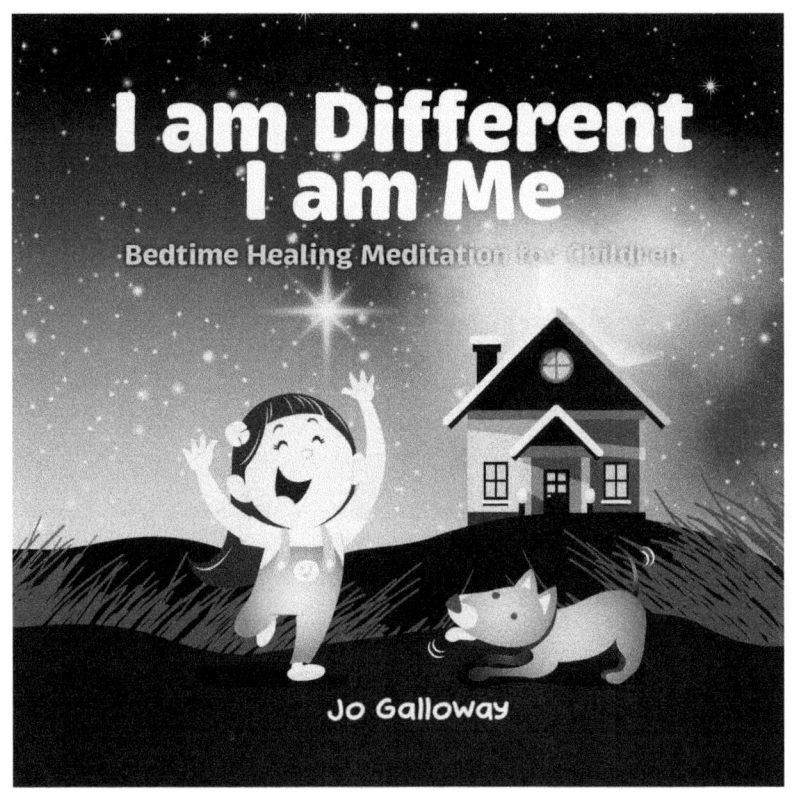

In a world where everyone is unique and special, being different is something to celebrate! "I Am Different, I Am Me" is a delightful bedtime story that shows just how wonderful it is to be yourself.

It's all about embracing our differences, celebrating our uniqueness, and feeling proud of who we are. This empowering meditation encourages your child to embrace their individuality and recognize their special gifts. They will discover the joy of being exactly who they were meant to be.

Give your child the gift of imagination and relaxation at bedtime with this easy-to-read story, designed to inspire and uplift.

Scared of the Dark

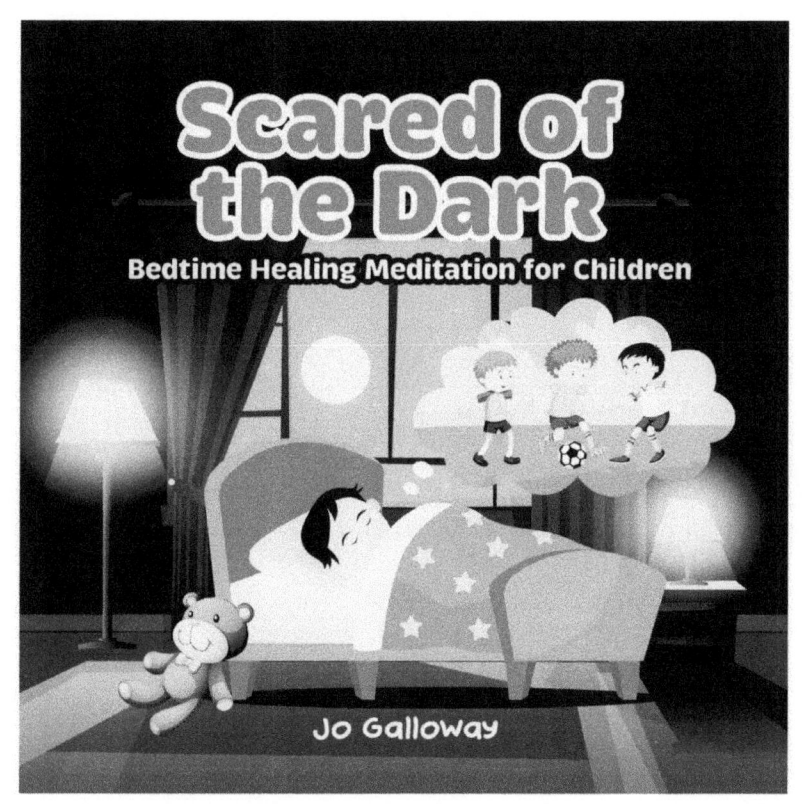

Join Teddy, your brave and comforting friend, on a magical bedtime journey designed to help little ones conquer their fears of the dark. In this gentle Healing Meditation, Teddy shares a heart warming story about overcoming night time worries and using the power of your imagination to transform fear into bravery. Through soothing guidance, deep breathing and a comforting countdown, Teddy helps children relax deeply and embrace their inner courage. Ideal for easing bedtime anxieties, this meditation fosters a sense of safety and confidence, ensuring a peaceful, restful night's sleep.

www.ingramcontent.com/pod-product-compliance
Lightning Source LLC
LaVergne TN
LVHW072054060526
838200LV00061B/4730